Fans Are Awesome

Written and illustrated by Samantha Seebeck

Fans are
awesome.

It's fun to watch them spin around and around.

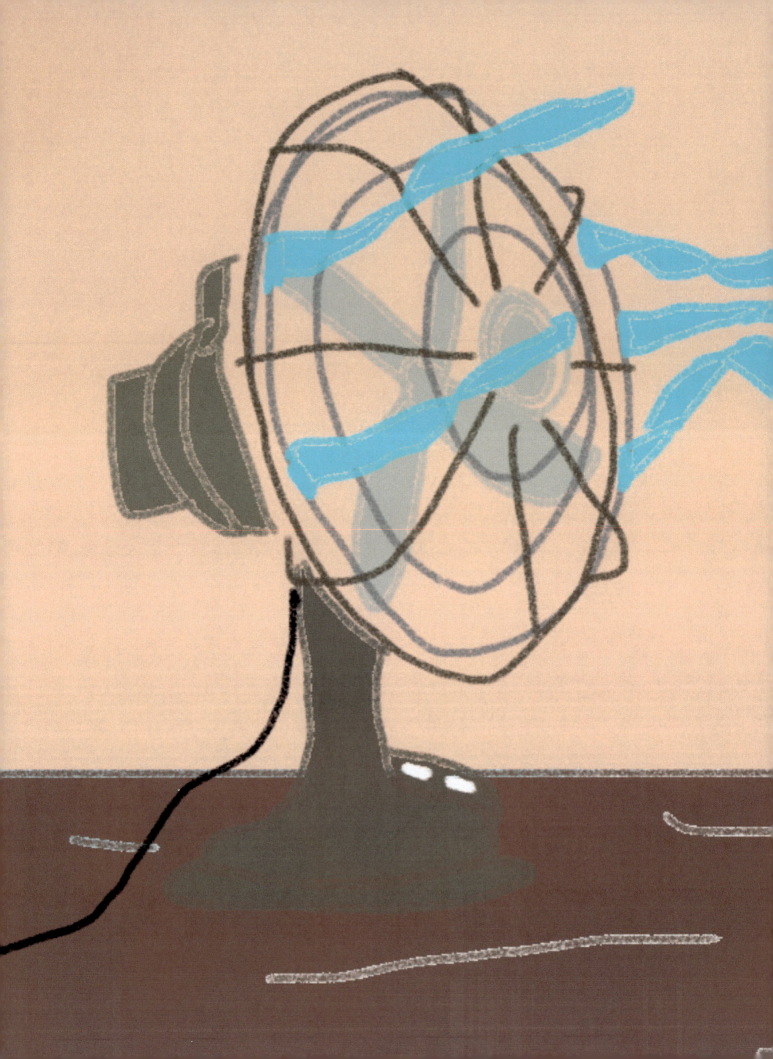

They keep you cool by creating a breeze.

And if you go ahhh into them it makes your voice sound funny.

(But only with a grown-up's help)

There are
ceiling fans.

Handheld fans.

And folding fans.

There are even huge fans called industrial fans for big, big spaces.

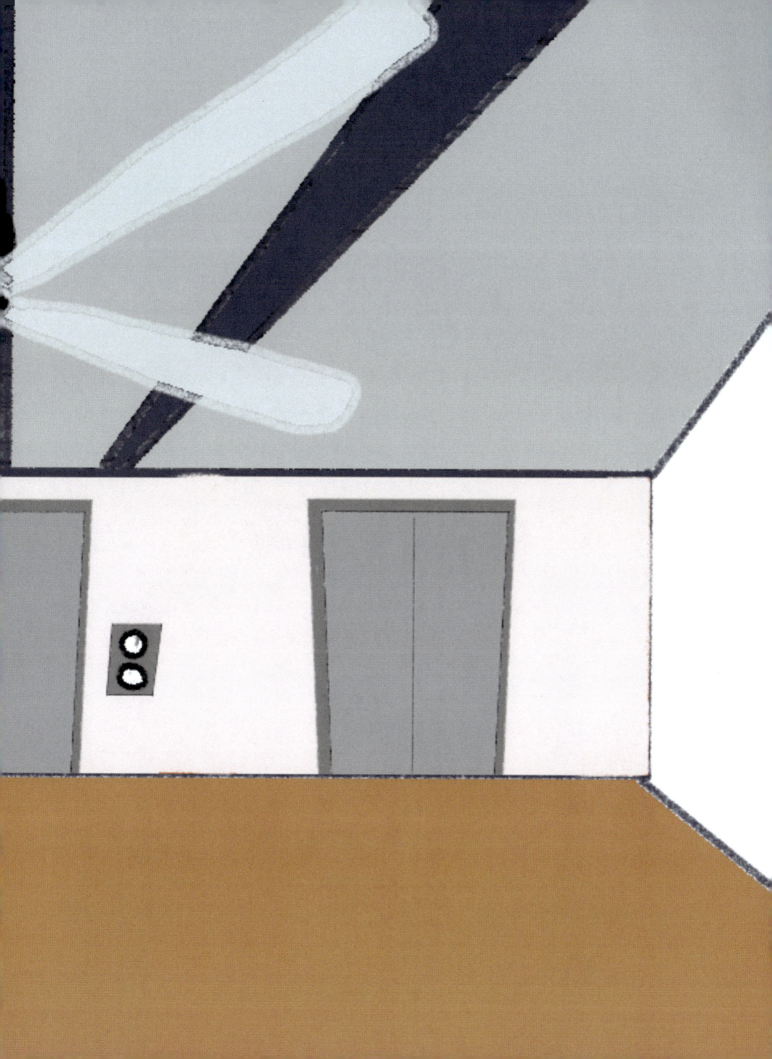

Fan

Fans have been keeping us cool for a long time, everywhere in the world. Here is a fan in Ancient Egypt.

Fans are used in all
kinds of dances,
like Flamenco dancing.

Fans are
awesome.

Do you think fans are awesome?

Made in the USA
Middletown, DE
02 July 2025